BERTRAND RUSSELL
&
TRINITY

G. H. HARDY

BERTRAND RUSSELL AND TRINITY

A facsimile reproduction
with a foreword by

C. D. BROAD

CAMBRIDGE
AT THE UNIVERSITY PRESS
1970

CAMBRIDGE UNIVERSITY PRESS
Cambridge, New York, Melbourne, Madrid, Cape Town, Singapore, São Paulo, Delhi

Cambridge University Press
The Edinburgh Building, Cambridge CB2 8RU, UK

Published in the United States of America by Cambridge University Press, New York

www.cambridge.org
Information on this title: www.cambridge.org/9780521113922

© Cambridge University Press 1970

First published 1970
This digitally printed version 2009

A catalogue record for this publication is available from the British Library

ISBN 978-0-521-07978-5 hardback
ISBN 978-0-521-11392-2 paperback

FOREWORD

Hardy's pamphlet *Bertrand Russell & Trinity* was written by him during the earlier years of the Second World War, and was completed towards the end of 1941. As stated in the Preface to it, it was printed for private circulation only. The printing was done for Hardy by the Cambridge University Press in 1942. When copies became available any Fellow of the College who wished to obtain one would find a pile of them on a table in the entrance-hall to Hardy's rooms. Alongside of them was a plate in which the intending purchaser would deposit his money, and a sheet of paper on which he would sign his name before taking away his purchase. A Fellow was allowed to buy more copies than one, and several of us did this in order to give them to friends who would thus learn the true account of a very complicated set of incidents. A copy of the pamphlet was preserved from the first in the Library of Trinity College, and it has always been available for consultation there by any of the Fellows who might care to inspect it.

From the above it will be plain that the pamphlet soon became something of a 'collector's piece'. Hardy died in 1947. He was survived by his sister, and after her death the copyright of all his writings passed to the London Mathematical Society. The latter, after consulting the College Council, now issues the pamphlet, with the Council's full approval, to the general public.

Besides being one of the most eminent pure mathematicians of his day, Hardy had a command of clear, elegant English, which makes anything that he wrote a pleasure to read. But in this pamphlet he excels, not only in this respect, but also in two others. The story of Russell's relations with Trinity during and immediately after the First World War is, as the reader will find, a highly complex one. It also involves matters on which Hardy had very definite opinions and very strong feelings. Now Hardy manages in a masterly way to disentangle the various incidents, and to enable the reader to see the connexions between them. And, while never attempting to conceal his own sentiments, he provides as fair and objective an account as is humanly possible of all the issues involved.

[*v*]

Hardy's pamphlet is the story of the breach between Russell and Trinity which occurred during the First World War. This resulted in Russell's severing his connexion with the College and taking his name off its books. As the reader will see, the breach was in fact healed by the end of 1919. On 12 December of that year the Council decided to offer to Russell a Lectureship in Logic and the Principles of Mathematics for five years from 1 July 1920, and on 16 January 1920 the Master was able to announce his acceptance.

But, although there was not and never has since been any further quarrel between Russell and the College, a set of unfortunate circumstances prevented this from becoming obvious to the world at large. Russell in fact, through his own action, never took up the Lectureship which the College had offered and which he had accepted. In the first place, in July 1920, just as his tenure was to have begun, he applied for leave of absence for the academic year 1920–21. This was granted, and he spent that period travelling and lecturing in China. Then, on 14 January 1921, he resigned the Lectureship, and his resignation was accepted. It was motivated, not by any difference with the College, but by circumstances in his private life which he feared might embarrass those who had supported his reinstatement.

That the breach really had been healed was shown later by the fact that in 1925 the Council invited Russell to give the Tarner Lectures, and that he accepted. The lectures which he then gave were afterwards published under the title *The Analysis of Matter*.

Hardy's pamphlet ends with the following sentence: "All the world of learning knows that there was a quarrel between the College and one of its most famous members: could it not be told, in language which leaves no possibility of misunderstanding, that the quarrel has since been healed?". Hardy's question did not long await a satisfactory answer. On 3 December 1943 the Council resolved to offer a Fellowship under Title B to Russell. The latter was then in the U.S.A., where he had been for some considerable time, and was planning in any case to return to England in the summer of 1944. He cabled his acceptance, and on 14 January 1944 the Council elected him to the promised Fellowship. The actual admission took place on 10 October 1944.

In reference to the above it should be explained that Trinity Fellowships, whilst uniform as regards qualifying the holder to vote at meetings of the Governing Body and to enjoy certain domestic privileges, are classified under certain Titles, which differ in regard to conditions of tenure and entitlement to stipend. A Fellowship under Title B is the rarest of these various categories. A Fellowship under it is given from time to time to a distinguished senior man. It confers on him a stipend subject only to the condition of his engaging in research.

In Russell's case the Council informed him that neither residence nor teaching would be required of him, but that the College would welcome it if he were inclined to lecture, and would pay a fee to him for such lecturing as he might be willing to undertake. On 28 July 1944 the Council agreed to invite Russell to lecture during the three academic years 1944–5, 1945–6, and 1946–7, and fixed the stipend for doing so. Russell did in fact lecture to large and enthusiastic audiences, and he resided in Cambridge (for part of the time in College) during much of the period. It was during this time that he put the finishing touches to his book *A History of Western Philosophy*.

The reader will see on pp. 48 *et seq.* of Hardy's pamphlet that the Fellow of the College who was mainly responsible in 1919 for the memorial which led to Russell's reinstatement was H. A. Hollond. It is of interest to record that it was the same Fellow (by that time Professor Hollond) who was primarily responsible for moving the Council to offer a Fellowship under Title B to Russell in 1944.

In October 1948 Russell's Fellowship under Title B was automatically coming to an end. On 1 October of that year the Council prolonged it until Michaelmas 1949. On the expiry of this prolonged Fellowship on 30 September 1949 Russell became automatically, under the Statutes, a Fellow under Title E. Such a Fellowship is tenable by the holder for the rest of his life, and accordingly Russell continued to be a Fellow under this title until his death on 2 February 1970.

In order to complete the story of Russell's relations with Trinity, I will end with a short summary of the relevant facts before 1919. He was admitted to the College on 17 June 1890. He took his B.A. degree in 1893, being seventh Wrangler in the Mathematical Tripos; and his M.A. degree in 1897. In 1895 he was awarded a Fellowship under the then Title (α). Such a Fellowship, popularly called a 'Prize Fellowship', was awarded as the result of an annual competition, at which each candidate submitted a dissertation on a subject chosen by himself.

It lasted for six years, and involved no duties of residence, research, or teaching. Russell was in fact away from Cambridge during the latter part of the period. The dissertation on which he won his Fellowship became the basis of his book *The Foundations of Geometry*. Finally, in 1910 the Council appointed Russell to a College Lectureship for five years in Logic and the Philosophy of Mathematics, which they created especially for him. Though it was not accompanied by a Fellowship Russell enjoyed many of the privileges of a Fellow, including rooms in College. He lectured, and he occupied rooms in Nevile's Court, from 1910 to the outbreak of war and somewhat later.

C. D. BROAD

Trinity College, Cambridge
25 *February* 1970

BERTRAND RUSSELL
&
TRINITY

A college controversy of the last war

BY

G. H. HARDY

Printed for the author
at the
UNIVERSITY PRESS
CAMBRIDGE

1942

[*ix*]

CONTENTS

v

PREFACE

This pamphlet is printed for private circulation only.

The College Council have given me permission to quote from sources (the Council Minutes, the Minutes of College Meetings, and the Report Book) accessible only to Fellows. I have also to thank Professor Broad, Mr Burnaby, Mrs A. Y. Campbell, Mr Hollond, Mr Laurence Housman, and Miss Parry for permission to reproduce letters.

I wish to make it plain that Russell himself is not responsible, directly or indirectly, for the writing of the pamphlet or for any of its contents. I wrote it without his knowledge and, when I sent him the typescript and asked for his permission to print it, I suggested that, unless it contained misstatements of fact, he should make no comment on it. He agreed to this course and, though I have altered it a good deal as the result of suggestions from other friends, no word has been changed as the result of any suggestion from him.

G. H. H.

Trinity College, Cambridge

4 *December* 1941

1. *Introduction*

The expulsion of Bertrand Russell from his lectureship in 1916 made a great stir at the time, and is still remembered as one of the minor sensations of the last war; but there are few men left, even in Trinity, who could tell the story of the case correctly. Outside the College there is hardly anyone who knows the facts at all, as I found in Oxford when I went there in 1920. Almost all my colleagues there were curious about the case and questioned me about it, and almost all of them had been wrong on four important points, about which misunderstanding was quite natural.

(1) It was generally believed that Russell had been deprived of a Fellowship. In fact he was not a Fellow, though he had been one, under title (α), from 1895 to 1901. It is of course much more difficult to remove a Fellow than to dismiss a lecturer.*

(2) It was supposed that he had been dismissed by the College acting as a whole, whereas actually he was dismissed by the Council. This is a very natural mistake for anyone unfamiliar with the constitution of a large college.

(3) It was supposed that he had been dismissed because he had been sent to prison. Actually, Russell was twice 'convicted of an offence', in 1916, when he was fined £100, and in 1918, when he was sentenced to six months' imprisonment. It was after the first conviction that he was dismissed; in 1918 he was no longer even a member of the College.

(4) Finally (and this was of course the most important misapprehension), no one knew·that he had ever been reinstated.

These misapprehensions made the action of the College

---

* See Statutes XIII and XXXIV (old Statutes XVII and XXXIV).

(or the Council) seem in some ways less, in some more, violent and irrational. Their net result was, I am sure, to discredit the College. By now every incident has been obscured still more by the passage of time; and I imagine that there are even many Fellows, elected during the last twenty years, who know as little about the affair as my Oxford colleagues knew in 1920. It therefore seems desirable, both to me and to friends whom I have consulted, that there should exist a coherent account of the whole matter, written by someone who really knows the facts, and accessible to every Fellow.

I have at any rate some of the qualifications for writing it. I did not take any part in the actual quarrel, except to sign the protest at the time and the memorial for Russell's reinstatement later; and indeed I had, in the peculiar conditions of the time, no opportunity of doing so. But I was here all through the war, and heard all there was to hear about the question (except, naturally, the private deliberations of the Council); I have discussed it with many members of the College whose opinions about it have differed widely; and I think that I have read nearly all the comments of any importance upon it which appeared in either the Cambridge or the London press. In any case it is likely that, if I do not write the story, no one will do so until it is too late.

There is one qualification which I certainly have not, though it may seem to some Fellows the most important: I am not 'impartial'. I felt bitterly about the matter at the time, and feel strongly about it still, and I have not changed my views on any important point. But I doubt if there is any Fellow who knows the facts, and has not, one way or the other, decided views about them. At any rate I will do my best to write dispassionately, and to make clear what is statement of fact and what is merely expression of my own feelings.

Actually, there will be five elements in my narrative. First, statements of fact published in the press, or otherwise generally accessible. Secondly, statements derived from confidential

2

sources (such as the Council Minutes and the Report Book) accessible only to Fellows. Thirdly, those based on what I have been told by other, past or present, Fellows. Fourthly, those for which I have to trust my own recollection. Finally, expressions of opinion. I will distinguish these various elements as carefully as I can.

2. *Public opinion towards pacifism during 1914–1918*

The emotions excited by pacifism* of all kinds during the last war were, except for short periods near its beginning and end, far more violent than they are now. In Cambridge, particularly, and above all in Trinity, there was often a real bitterness which a present Fellow may find it difficult to picture. It is impossible to understand the Russell case without understanding something of the reasons for this intensity of feeling, and I must begin by saying something about those which underlay general public opinion.

(1) It must be remembered, first, that there was much more genuine political disagreement about the last war than there has been about this one.

(2) There was no automatic conscription: conscription came gradually and after a big fight. First there was the

---

* I use the words 'pacifism' and 'pacifist', here and later, in the sense in which they came gradually to be used by the public and the press during 1914–1918, that is to say as applicable to all individuals and organizations whose views about the war were in any way unorthodox or unpopular. Thus I should describe Russell, Lowes Dickinson, Ramsay MacDonald, Lord Lansdowne (after 1916), and indeed anybody who did not accept the doctrine of 'victory at all costs', as 'pacifists', and I shall call the 'U.D.C.' a 'pacifist organization'. The word degenerated into a term of abuse, and I have no doubt that many people whom I should call pacifists would have repudiated the description, and reserved the word for those who subscribed to particular doctrines about the wickedness of war and the sanctity of human life. The implications of the word have no doubt moved in this direction since 1918; but I need a word to use in the sense which I have explained, and cannot find a better one.

3

period of enthusiasm and of genuinely voluntary enlistment; then the period of voluntary enlistment under the pressure of public opinion, or economic pressure; finally, in the dying days of the voluntary system, the period of the 'Derby scheme'.* There was no attempt, in the early stages, at systematic reservation, though certain classes, such as munition workers and civil servants over a certain age, came gradually to be reserved in practice. A man's decision to join up depended entirely upon his sense of duty, his sensitiveness to public opinion, and the attitude of his employer.

(3) The 'tribunal' system caused great bitterness after the coming of conscription. Apart from munition workers and a few other privileged classes, every man who wanted exemption, or whose employer wanted it for him, had to state his case individually to a tribunal. These tribunals dealt with appeals of all kinds. A man might appeal on the ground of special hardship, on the ground that his work was of national importance, on conscientious or even on medical grounds; whatever the ground, he went before the same tribunal, and his case was reported in the press.

The working of the system depended entirely on the personality of the tribunals, and above all of their chairmen. The Cambridge tribunal contained representatives of the University, and was no doubt one of the best; but many were both stupid and brutal, and could not be trusted to carry out correctly even the letter of the law or of the instructions which they received from time to time. And naturally all the weaknesses of the tribunal system were shown up most clearly by their treatment of conscientious objectors.

(4) Pacifist organizations were more numerous, more combative, and more diverse, both in their avowed aims and in their underlying motives (which were by no means always

* Under which, certainly, hundreds of thousands 'volunteered' because they regarded conscription as certain and supposed (quite wrongly) that voluntary attestation would entitle them to preferential treatment. I can say this the more easily as a 'Derby man' myself.

4

the same). There were two which are particularly important for my purpose, the U.D.C. (Union of Democratic Control) and the N.C.F. (No Conscription Fellowship) : of these I shall have a good deal more to say later. There were also the I.L.P., which was definitely political, but had many members in common with the U.D.C. and the N.C.F., the National Council against Conscription (to organize political opposition to conscription before it came), and a good many definitely religious bodies such as the Friends' Service Committee. All of these bodies, except the U.D.C. and the I.L.P., came gradually to be occupied more and more with cases of hardship to conscientious objectors. For the properly political pacifist, naturally, the conscientious objector was always a handicap which he had to carry.

(5) Finally, there was no 'total' war; a general at the War Office, a bellicose civilian, or a conscientious objector who had been given total exemption, could carry on their work in almost complete safety.*

I should add a word about the *official* attitude towards pacifists, and particularly conscientious objectors, though it cannot be more than a statement of my personal opinion. I have always thought that the Government's policy was, granted the premises from which it started, and considering the great difficulties of the problem, on the whole very reasonable. They had, on the one hand, to avoid any serious loss of military efficiency or man-power, on the other to do their best to conciliate bitterly hostile currents of public opinion. If there were scandals—and there were many bad ones—it was not primarily the fault of the central authorities. We should remember that the internment of aliens in this war led to a good deal of hardship and injustice, and reflect that, then as now, the carrying out of the intentions of the Government was often in the hands of subordinates who,

* The total number of deaths from air-raids during the war was 1414 (670 in London).

5

deliberately or from sheer stupidity, failed to give effect to their orders.

As regards conscientious objectors, the position was roughly as follows.

(*a*) It was admitted by all except a few extremists that some recognition of conscientious objection was inevitable. Only a negligible minority were prepared for a religious persecution.

(*b*) It was also admitted, by all except a few extremists on the other side, that, while the majority of conscientious objectors were honest, and some of them very estimable people, there was a substantial body of would-be 'shirkers' prepared, if the way were made at all easy for them, to become conscientious objectors in order to escape military service. It was therefore essential, on military as well as on political grounds, that the position of a conscientious objector should be a hard and unpleasant one.

(*c*) It was certain that the decisions of the Government would often be administered by quite unintelligent and violently prejudiced agents. The result would be that, whether a conscientious objector were honest or not, his chance of securing exemption, and the nature of that exemption, would often depend on external circumstances, and in particular on his education, his social position, and the pressure that could be exerted by his friends. Indeed all this is true to some extent even under the much more rational system in force to-day.

All this must have been familiar to the Government; and their policy in the circumstances seemed to me then, and seems still, fundamentally sane. They wanted the position of a conscientious objector to carry with it penalties just sufficient to deter all but completely honest or very determined men.

The Government (at any rate its more prominent and intelligent members) never wished to *attack* pacifists, and least of all those who were obviously honest, able, and determined. And the last thing they could have wanted would have been to attack so formidable an antagonist as Russell, a man who was famous all over the world, and particularly in America, and whose prosecution would be bound to provoke a first-class sensation. They prosecuted Russell because, first the stupidity of their agents, then his own challenge, made prosecution inevitable.

On the other hand I imagine that there is no doubt that, once having begun the prosecution, they were quite determined that it should succeed. I was told at the time that a good deal of influence was brought to bear on the Lord Mayor, when he showed signs of being too much impressed by Russell's arguments. I cannot substantiate this assertion, but it is very plausible, since Russell argued well and an *unsuccessful* prosecution would have been disastrous.

I should add that all that I have said about public opinion applies particularly to the first three years of the war. It had toned down a good deal before the end of 1917, most people having become, in private, exhausted and rather cynical.*

3. *Opinion in the College*

There were additional causes tending to exacerbate feeling in Cambridge, and particularly in Trinity.

(1) In the last war there was no automatic 'reservation' of dons, though the University or a College could appeal for the exemption of a teacher if they regarded him as 'indispensable'. Nor was there, at any rate in the early stages

* It is hardly too much to say that, late in the war, the respect shown to one by a porter, taxi-driver, or waiter was *greater* if one was not in uniform: it was evidence that one was really a 'toff'. I can recall a rather amusing case of this in my own experience. I had shared lodgings with a friend for a year or so in Eaton Terrace, but some time in 1917 he left and I had to find other rooms. I had always gone out before breakfast to buy the *Morning Post* from a news-vendor at the corner, and when I went out on the last day I said to him 'I'm afraid this is the last time I shall be buying a paper from you'. I shall never forget the sudden look of disillusionment in his eyes, or the tone in which he said ' *What*, Sir, they've not nabbed *you*, Sir?' He may of course have spoken ironically.

7

of the war, any real attempt to use scientific ability systematically: thus Littlewood was an artillery officer and
Fowler a marine (though both were turned to scientific work
later). The result was a sweeping clearance from Cambridge
of dons below a certain age, and a corresponding concentra-
tion of the government of the College in the hands of the
senior Fellows.

(2) There was a clearly defined 'minority' in the College.
Four Fellows were conscientious objectors, and thirteen members of the U.D.C. (though four of these held commissions in
the Army). These Fellows formed a party whose views, though
by no means identical, were in sharp conflict with those of
the majority and in particular with those of the Council; and
no member of this minority would have stood the slightest
chance of election to the Council. Thus membership of the
Council became more and more the prerogative of the senior
Fellows, and it is no wonder that it should have gradually
lost touch with the general opinion of the College.

(3) The minority included a number of 'provocative'
people, though no one who was actually a Fellow in 1916 was
at all prominent publicly.*

(4) There was a strong feeling among the senior Fellows
that Cambridge was regarded by the world outside as a
stronghold of pacifism. This feeling was no doubt exag-
gerated, but it is undeniable that there was something in it,
and that the suspicion with which Cambridge was regarded
was due primarily to Russell.† There was a sharp contrast
in this respect between Cambridge and Oxford, which never
had a similar reputation, and where differences of opinion
were much more successfully controlled or concealed.

---

* The most prominent people were Russell himself (a lecturer absent on
leave) and Barnes (who had ceased to be a Fellow a little before).

† Lowes Dickinson was also suspect as a pacifist; but he was less provocative
than Russell, and devoted himself more and more, as the war went on, to
'League of Nations' propaganda. See Ch. XII of E. M. Forster's *Goldsworthy
Lowes Dickinson*.

There was another important factor in the reputation of Cambridge, *The Cambridge Magazine*, a remarkable journal very ably edited by C. K. Ogden. The *Cambridge Magazine* was founded in 1912, and was certainly the most interesting 'undergraduate' periodical ever produced in either University. It acquired a considerable outside circulation during the war, mainly as the result of an excellent 'survey of foreign opinion' edited by Mrs C. R. Buxton: this part of the *Magazine* came out weekly even during vacations, and was almost the only place where one could find an impartial selection of what was appearing in the foreign press. Naturally it had to face much hostility, which was fomented vigorously by various senior members of the University; but it continued as a weekly until 1920, and as a quarterly until 1923. Its premises in King's Parade and Bridge Street were smashed up during the riots in 'Armistice Week', but I need not go into that discreditable story.

The *Cambridge Magazine* was not an avowedly pacifist organ, but there was never any doubt about which side its sympathies lay. In particular, during the early days of conscription, it gave full reports of the proceedings at tribunals when prominent conscientious objectors appeared before them. These ceased after the Russell case: 'it is always our policy to stop short of anything likely to promote prosecution or raids.' But the *Magazine* was, as we shall see, very outspoken in its comments on the action of the Council.

For all these reasons feeling in Trinity had become tense long before the Russell case: it was plain, all through 1915, that the clouds were banking up for a storm. The relations between Fellows never degenerated to the point of downright rudeness, but different sections definitely avoided one another.* The general tension reached its height in the summer of 1916, after Russell's dismissal, and did not develop further:

* Rather as Dickinson and McTaggart, who had been most intimate friends, avoided one another.

9

I can hardly remember a reference to the second Russell case of 1918. But life in College was through all these years, for a member of the minority, definitely unpleasant, and the recollection of them was an important factor in my own decision to try to move to Oxford.

The storm broke first over a dispute which seemed a minor affair after Russell's dismissal, and in which he was not involved directly. I shall begin my narrative of events in College with the story of this dispute, but I must first say a little more about the U.D.C. and the N.C.F., the two pacifist organizations over which our quarrels came to a head.

4. *The U.D.C.*

The Union of Democratic Control was founded shortly after the beginning of the war. Its first manifesto, a letter to the press signed by Norman (now Sir Norman) Angell, Ramsay MacDonald, E. D. Morel and C. P. (now Sir Charles) Trevelyan (who had resigned from the Government in August), appeared in September 1914; and its first pamphlet, *The Morrow of the War*, in October. It had a General Council of thirty members, the most conspicuous of whom (besides the four whom I have mentioned already) were H. N. Brailsford, Arthur Henderson, Arthur Ponsonby (now Lord Ponsonby of Shulbrede), Russell, and Lees Smith. Morel, a remarkable man famous for his part in the exposure of the 'Congo atrocities', was honorary secretary and treasurer. Philip Snowden (afterwards Viscount Snowden) joined later. All these men represented what were then the left wings of the Liberal and Labour parties; and a good many of the members of the Union were, or became later, Members of Parliament, and formed the intellectual nucleus of the first Labour

Government of 1924. There was a Cambridge branch, of which Dickinson was president* and I was secretary. The U.D.C. was not originally a particularly 'unorthodox' body. *The Morrow of the War* (a very ably written document, like most of its publications) contains a statement, with the necessary expansions, of the Union's four main 'planks'; and these are all based on the assumptions, then made by almost everybody, that the war must be won, and will be won fairly quickly. The Union is to concern itself solely with the settlement after the war.

We believe that all are in agreement about two things. First, it is imperative that the war, once begun, should be prosecuted to a victory for our country. Secondly, it is equally imperative, while we carry on the war, to prepare for peace....

The Union of Democratic Control has been created to insist that the following policy shall inspire the actual conditions of peace, and shall dominate the situation after peace has been declared:—

1. No Province shall be transferred from one Government to another without the consent, by plebiscite or otherwise, of the population of such Province.

2. No Treaty, Arrangement, or Undertaking shall be entered upon in the name of Great Britain without the sanction of Parliament. Adequate machinery for ensuring democratic control of foreign policy shall be created....

It is this second plank, of course, to which the founders of the Union attached particular importance and from which they drew its name. It is something of a departure from 'orthodoxy', since it implies criticism of the 'understandings' with France before 1914. The third plank is rather vaguer: foreign policy is to be aimed, not at a 'balance of power', but at 'concerted action between the Powers and the setting up of an International Council': this is a vague foreshadowing of

* Dickinson became absorbed in the League of Nations Society later, and a little out of sympathy with the U.D.C., though he never resigned from it. See Forster, *l.c.*, pp. 168–169.

11

the League of Nations. Finally, the fourth plank deals with disarmament and nationalisation of the armament industry. Later, a fifth point, 'no economic war after the war', was added to the programme.

The programme is, at first sight, thoroughly 'respectable'. There is little in it likely to shock anyone except a very pronounced right-winger; and, except for the general suspicion of 'highbrows' and 'cranks' which is inevitable in war time, the Union did not seem to be particularly unpopular. The difficulty was rather to interest people in it; but Cambridge, as might have been expected, proved to be one of its best recruiting grounds. The first public meeting of the Cambridge Branch was held in the Guildhall on 4 March 1915, Morel being the principal speaker and Barnes in the chair. There was no excitement or protest of any kind, and the meeting was tolerably successful. The attendance was not enough to encourage us to try another meeting in a large hall; but we held a good many smaller meetings, and found no difficulty in hiring or borrowing rooms.

As the war went on and opinion became steadily more bitter—in particular, as conscription approached—the U.D.C. gradually became unpopular: there were a good many attacks on it in the more extreme press, and disturbances at meetings in London and other large towns. It is inevitable that any body primarily interested in peace should become unpopular in time of war, but in this case it is easy to pick out special reasons.

(1) The U.D.C. contained an unusual proportion of men who, however reasonable their views might be, and however ably they might express them, had in a high degree the knack of exasperating their opponents. This was true, for example, of MacDonald, of Snowden (who was often very bitter), of Russell himself, and of Morel. It was particularly true of Morel, who was regarded, probably rightly, as the first force in the Union. Morel was an aggressive controversialist who

had distinguished himself in many fights, and especially in those about the Belgian Congo. For his share in that fight he had received much honour at the time, but it was all turned against him now; only 'Germany's agent'* could ever have criticized Belgian administration.

(2) Although the U.D.C. itself was not concerned with conscientious objectors, a number of members were active on their behalf, both before and after conscription; and a good many became conscientious objectors themselves.

(3) There was a general suspicion that many members of the U.D.C. were gradually shifting their ground, and really stood for something which did not appear in their statements of policy.

This last point is much the most important; and I will say at once that the feeling that the U.D.C. 'really meant something different' was to a considerable extent justified (though in a way which most of the people who attacked it would probably have been quite unable to express). I can verify this by recalling the development of my own opinions; and I have no doubt that those of many other members changed gradually in much the same way.

It was obvious by the autumn of 1915 that the naive assumptions about military victory, on which the original programme had been based, were entirely mistaken. For my own part (and I am sure that I represented a large body of

* *Evening Standard*, 7 July 1917. The *Morning Post* and the *New Witness* had referred to Morel in similar terms long before.

The prejudice against Morel, and in particular against his activities about the Congo, was increased by an unlucky coincidence. The other British subject who had done most to expose the Congo atrocities was Sir Roger Casement, the author of the famous official report on the Upper Congo in 1903; and Casement, to Morel's consternation, joined hands with Germany during the war.

Morel was sentenced to six months' imprisonment on 4 September 1917 for, roughly, sending pacifist literature out of the country: the actual charge was more complicated. There is a verbatim report of the case (which had a rather discreditable history behind it, though no doubt the verdict was technically correct) in *Rex* v. *E. D. Morel* (U.D.C. pamphlets, no. 24 a). See also Lord Snowden's *Autobiography*, vol. I, pp. 423-4.

opinion in the Union) I had gone to the opposite extreme. I had become convinced (a) that military victory, in the sense in which it actually came in 1918, was impossible, and (b) that if it came it would be a disaster. In short, I had become a 'Lansdownian', long before the publication of Lord Lansdowne's famous letter, and so, no doubt, had a considerable proportion of the members of the U.D.C. Now Lansdownism, a drawn war and a compromise peace, was certainly not part of the declared policy of the Union, and indeed verbally contradicted it; so that the suspicion of the public that the U.D.C. really 'stood for something else' was by no means altogether unjustified.

It was not surprising that the Council should have shared this general suspicion, and have felt nervous about the association of so many Fellows with the Union. Might it not have really serious effects on the future of the College? Would parents, after the war, send their sons to a College thus tainted? This anxiety, very natural although as events proved entirely mistaken, was expressed in so many words by Lapsley in his speech at the College Meeting to which I am coming.

I will add a few words (though they are not strictly relevant) about the later history of the U.D.C. Its unpopularity grew steadily up to the time of Morel's imprisonment in 1917, but it was always strictly 'legal' and, though often 'raided', was never suppressed. For a long time it was a struggling as well as an unpopular body, always in need of funds, but this was changed dramatically in 1918. In November 1917 the Russian Revolutionary Government published the secret treaties found in the archives of the Russian Foreign Office. An outline of them was printed in the *Manchester Guardian* a little later; and in April 1918 the U.D.C. published *The Secret Treaties and Understandings*, a full text with notes and maps, compiled by Seymour Cocks. This book made a great sensation and had a very large sale, which effectively consolidated the Union's finances.

After the war, the Union became thoroughly 'respectable'. Almost all its M.P.'s lost their seats in 1918, but were returned again in 1924 or in previous by-elections. Most of those who became members of the Government then resigned from the Union, but it continued its activities and still survives.*

5. The N.C.F.

The first storm in College was over the U.D.C. Russell was not involved in this directly, since he was not a Fellow (though it is essential that I should give an account of it, if we are to understand what happened later). The Russell case originated in the activities of the N.C.F.; and I had better say something about this body also before I begin my story of events in College.

The No Conscription Fellowship was a much less 'intellectual' body than the U.D.C. It was founded in October 1914, with Clifford Allen (afterwards Lord Allen of Hurtwood) as chairman, and Fenner Brockway and Aylmer Rose as secretaries. Its first purpose was to fight conscription by parliamentary methods; but it always contemplated resistance to military service if conscription was enforced, and for this reason its membership was limited to men of military age. A very large proportion of the members were drawn from the Society of Friends and other definitely religious bodies, and practically all of them became conscientious objectors after conscription. By September 1916 the N.C.F. had a membership of between 15,000 and 20,000.†

The best statement of the motives of the N.C.F. is to be found in Clifford Allen's presidential address to the 'National

* As a mildly advanced organization primarily interested in foreign policy. Its journal is now called *Foreign Affairs* (but has not appeared for some time).

† See *The N.C.F.: a record of its activities*, published on 2 September 1916. There is a considerable collection of N.C.F. pamphlets in the University Library: this includes the 'Everett' leaflet which caused Russell's prosecution.

Convention' held on 27 November 1915 (when conscription, though not actually law, was practically certain). He described it as

an organization of men who will refuse from conscientious motives to bear arms, because they consider human life to be sacred....

The N.C.F. will

oppose every effort to introduce compulsory service. Should such efforts be successful they will, whatever the consequences may be, obey their conscientious convictions....

He went on

You can oppose a Bill in the House of Commons, and by agitation...up to the time that that Bill becomes law.... You can also resist the operations of that Act, should it go on the Statute Book. I want it to be clearly known here, speaking on behalf of the Fellowship, that it is the latter of these two kinds of opposition that we intend to offer....

Whatever ambiguity there may have been in the objects of the U.D.C., it must be admitted that there was none at all in those of the N.C.F.; and it must be admitted also that a very large proportion of its members were as good as their word, and did exactly what they said they were going to do.

After the passage of the Military Service Act, the N.C.F. had to concentrate on the advice and support of conscientious objectors and the exposure of scandals concerning them. There were a good many leaflets about individual cases, of which the Everett case was typical. The N.C.F. also published *The Court-Martial Friend and Prison Guide*, a detailed statement about procedure at courts-martial, prison rules, and so on: this is a sensible and temperately written document.

Naturally the N.C.F. was in continual trouble, and there were many raids and prosecutions. Thus on 18 May 1916, just before the Russell case, a number of officials of the N.C.F. were prosecuted on a similar charge, that of circulating a leaflet *Repeal the Act* in a manner likely to 'prejudice recruiting and discipline'. They included the treasurer

(Edward Grubb) and one of the secretaries (Fenner Brockway), but not Clifford Allen or C. H. Norman, who were 'serving in the Army' (i.e. in prison by sentence of courts-martial). All of them were fined £100; some, including Brockway, refused to pay their fines and went to prison. There were a good many similar prosecutions of officials both of the N.C.F. and other bodies;* but the organization was never actually suppressed, and still existed at the end of 1918.

There was only one occasion, apart from the Russell case, when the N.C.F. created a stir in academic circles in Cambridge.† The story is trivial, but I cannot resist the temptation of telling it.

Mr R. H. Macleod was a retired Indian civilian who was employed by the University to give instruction in Indian Law to I.C.S. probationers, and had been given an honorary M.A. He was an unimportant person, but became a little notorious during the war for his 'pacifist-hunting' activities, and was one of the people responsible for the attacks on the offices of the *Cambridge Magazine*.

Mr Macleod suspected that there was a branch of the N.C.F. in Cambridge, and wished to make trouble for it; but it had done nothing public and he did not know who were its officials. The central office in London had made it known that it would give advice to intending conscientious objectors, and this suggested to him the following ingenious scheme. He wrote a letter to the London office in the name of 'J. R. Smith', representing himself as a conscientious objector who did not know the proper procedure, and asking for advice. The London office, as he had calculated, forwarded the letter to the secretary of the Cambridge Branch, who was actually a Trinity undergraduate. 'Mr Smith' had stated that he was a gardener who could not leave his employment, and that he

* Thus three officials of the Friends' Service Committee were sent to prison on 25 May 1918 for publishing a leaflet 'likely to be used for propaganda purposes' without submitting it to the Press Bureau.

† See the *Cambridge Magazine*, 4 March 1916 and succeeding numbers.

17

would be grateful if some agent of the N.C.F. would come to see him at his address: this, naturally, was Mr Macleod's. The secretary and a friend accordingly went there, where they were confronted by Mr Macleod himself, who produced his Special Constable's warrant and arrested them. They were then taken to the Police Station, and detained for three hours while a constable was sent to search their rooms. They were, however, allowed to telephone to their Tutor, and it was then discovered that, since all the purposes of the N.C.F. were strictly legal, there was no charge that could be brought against them and no excuse for further detention. The affair naturally caused a good deal of rather acid comment, but Mr Macleod apparently continued to regard his part in it with satisfaction. It has a certain interest as an indication of feeling in Cambridge.*

6. *The Council and the U.D.C.*

The Cambridge Branch of the U.D.C. held a number of meetings during 1914–1915, sometimes in rooms in the town hired for the occasion and sometimes in College rooms. We did not try to arrange another public meeting after the meeting in the Guildhall. Meetings were limited to members and their friends; but we usually tried to get a speaker from outside, and the times of meetings were announced in the *Magazine*.

The issue of 13 November 1915 printed the notice:

The Annual General Meeting will be held on Thursday, 25 Nov. at 8.30 p.m. in Mr J. E. Littlewood's rooms, D Nevile's Court, Trinity College. Mr Charles Roden Buxton will speak on 'Nationality and the Settlement'.

* Actually the *Magazine*, in its comments on the case, made a statement for which Mr Macleod was able to enforce an apology. It had stated that he had 'sent a bogus letter to an undergraduate', and that was false: he had sent a bogus letter to a person, not an undergraduate, who had forwarded it to an undergraduate.

Mr Buxton (a former Scholar of Trinity) was a recognized authority on the Balkans, and it was about this side of the 'settlement' that he intended to speak. Littlewood was absent on military service, but he was a member, and had given written permission for the meeting. We had held several previous meetings of the Branch in his rooms, because they were standing empty and were much larger and more convenient than mine.

I was naturally much astonished when Mr Ogden came to see me on the night of 19 November, when all the arrangements for the meeting had been completed, and showed me a letter which had been sent him for publication in his next issue.

Trinity College, 19 Nov. 1915

Sir,

With reference to an announcement contained in the last issue of the *Cambridge Magazine*, I am desired by the Council of Trinity College to request you to publish the following order which was made by the Council at their meeting to-day:

'That no meeting of the Union of Democratic Control be held within the precincts of the College.'

I remain,

Yours faithfully,

H. McLeod Innes, Secretary of the Council.

This letter appeared next day, together with a statement of my own:

I have received no official communication from the Council of Trinity College concerning the proposed meeting of the Union of Democratic Control, and am surprised that their resolution should have been communicated first to the Press.*

I do not know whether the Council have legal power to prohibit a Fellow of the College from holding a meeting in his rooms. The question of the wisdom of their action, as

---

* I do not suppose that the Council wished to be deliberately rude: they had to act hurriedly, since the *Magazine* came out on the day after the Council Meeting. But I never received any explanation of any kind.

distinct from its legality, is one about which I shall have other opportunities of expressing my opinion.

The meeting will be held in the Assembly Rooms, Downing Street.

Actually, the meeting was never held. On 24 November we received a letter from the Chairman of the Committee of the Liberal Club, who were the tenants of the rooms, cancelling the engagement on the ground of 'the existence of a feeling that the holding of the meeting would be contrary to the national welfare'. They had let us have the rooms before, and their action was obviously suggested by that of the Council. It was then too late to make new arrangements, and the meeting had to be abandoned. On 27 November our Committee published a statement, recapitulating the facts, but naturally adding that 'the legality and the advisability of the action of the Council is of course a matter for the College to pronounce upon'. Later, the *Magazine* printed a number of letters, but nothing worth quoting here.

One member of the Council, Rouse Ball, had voted against the resolution.* He was no 'pacifist', but a staunch individualist, and regarded it as an unwarrantable interference with the rights of Fellows. I consulted him and James Ward, who was more definitely in sympathy with me, and we decided to call a College Meeting by requisition. We did not expect to find any difficulty in getting the necessary number of signatures, but we had no illusions about the result: we were certain to be outvoted, if only because so many of our probable supporters would be absent.

I have a copy of the flysheet which I circulated before the

---

* It was moved That no meeting of the Union of Democratic Control be held within the precincts of the College. The motion was carried by 8 votes to 1. Mr Ball voted against the motion (*Minutes of the Council*, 19 November 1915).

The members present were the Master (Montagu Butler), the Vice-Master (Jackson), Stanton, Ball, Parry, McTaggart, Whetham (now Sir William Dampier), Innes, Laurence, and Dykes. There was one abstention (I believe Stanton).

meeting,* and still find it rather amusing reading, though it was a good deal softened by my senior and more judicious advisers. After a statement of the facts, I went on—

The first question which suggests itself is that of the legal power of the Council to prohibit a Fellow from holding a meeting of a society in his rooms. This is not the point on which I wish to lay stress. It is arguable that such a power exists. The Council has power, under Statute XLII. 5, 'to make orders for the good government of the College, and for maintaining and improving the discipline and studies of the students thereof'. This provision might conceivably be held legally to justify almost any action on the part of the Council.†
...The important question is in any case not whether the Council does or does not possess such powers, but whether, assuming that it does, the Fellows as a whole regard its action in using them in this manner as wise and reasonable. I am sure that I can appeal with confidence to Fellows of the College to consider this question on its merits;‡ not to allow their judgement to be prejudiced by any dislike of the activities of the Union; and to remember that, if to be a Fellow of Trinity means anything, it means that a Fellow has the right and power to say what he thinks, whether or no his opinions are those of the majority of his countrymen, and even if they differ from those of the Council.

I can imagine circumstances in which action similar to the present action of the Council might be defensible. If I proposed to hold a meeting in my rooms for a purpose admittedly seditious, the Council might be right in passing a resolution to forbid me....

My original draft here ran (I have to trust to my memory):
'If I proposed to hold a meeting in my rooms for a purpose admittedly seditious, *for example to discuss plans for the assassina-*

* Those were the days of 'flysheets', both in University and College controversies.
† The legal question still seems to me genuinely interesting. I consulted Mr C. P. Sanger (a former Fellow) at the time, and he advised me that it seemed to him very doubtful. He added that there was no doubt at all that the decision would go against me *then*, especially since Mr Justice Darling was intensely 'anti-pacifist' and would certainly insist on trying the case himself. Of course I had no serious intention of taking legal action.
‡ I cannot believe now that I was really quite so innocent.

tion of the King, the Council might be right in passing a resolution to forbid me, *though I should have supposed that it would be more sensible to send for the police.'* Ball and Ward were no doubt right in insisting that I should omit the words italicized, though I regret it now.

I ended with a demand that some spokesman of the Council should state its reasons for its action formally; but there is nothing else that I need quote.

7. *The College Meeting about the U.D.C.*

The requisition was signed by 22 Fellows, namely

Ball	Eddington	Norton	Chapman
Ward	Littlewood	Gow	Fowler
Barnes	Hollond	Neville	D. H. Robertson
Cornford	D. S. Robertson	Broad	Proudman
Hardy	Hopkins	Southwell	
Winstanley	Watson	Tennant	

Two further signatures, those of G. I. Taylor and Adrian, were received after the requisition had been presented.* A Special College Meeting was therefore summoned. Minutes of College Meetings have a very characteristic eloquence, and I will allow this set to tell their own story.

Minutes of the Special College Meeting held on 22 January 1916

Present the Master and 44 Fellows.
1. The minutes of the College Meeting held 6 Feb. 1915 and of the meeting of the Master and Fellows being Graduates held 27 May 1915 were read and confirmed.
2. Dr Ward (seconded by Mr Ball) moved the following resolution of which notice had been given in the requisition:
That in the opinion of this meeting a Fellow of the College should be entitled to receive in his rooms as guests members

* On the other hand one or two signatories ceased to be Fellows before the meeting.

22

of a society invited to promote its objects, these being neither illegal nor immoral.

Sir J. J. Thomson (seconded by Dr Whitehead) moved as an amendment

That the word 'privately' be inserted between the words 'society' and 'invited'.

The proposer and seconder of the original resolution signified their willingness to accept the amendment by leave of the meeting.

The motion that leave be given was carried by 41 votes to 2. The Vice-Master voted against the motion.

Mr Lapsley (seconded by Mr H. M. Taylor) moved as an amendment

To add at the end of the resolution the words 'provided the interests of the College are not prejudiced thereby'.

The votes were Ayes 28, Noes 14. The amendment was therefore carried.

On the motion as amended Dr Fletcher (seconded by Mr Hicks) moved

That the question be not put.

The votes were Ayes 25, Noes 11. The motion was therefore carried.

The meeting then ended.

Not very much comment is necessary.

(1) The Fellows present were

The Vice-Master	Jenkinson	Whetham	Eddington
(Jackson)	Frazer	Capstick	Littlewood
Prior	Thomson	Innes	Newall
H. M. Taylor	Parry	Fletcher	Hopkins
Image	Herman	Cornford	Watson
Kirkpatrick	Duff	Harrison	G. I. Taylor
Stanton	Whitehead	Hardy	Norton
Boughey	Langley	Laurence	Neville
Ball	Bevan	Lapsley	Tennant
Ward	Cunningham	Lucas	Chapman
Hicks	McTaggart	Dykes	Adrian
Glazebrook			

It was a surprisingly large meeting.

(2) The tactics were interesting. The first amendment surrendered a little, but nothing worth fighting about. The

23

two who voted against it presumably thought that its acceptance would improve the prospects of the motion.

(3) The crucial division was that on Lapsley's amendment. This practically converted the motion into a vote of
confidence in the Council, encouraging them to prohibit
anything which they judged prejudicial to 'the interests of
the College'. Our party would of course have voted solidly
against the amended motion, if it had actually been put to
the meeting.

(4) I do not like motions to shelve discussion.* But in this
case Fletcher's motion was probably the best solution, and
Ward, Ball, and I all voted for it. We felt certain that the
motion, as amended, would have been carried.

(5) My own most vivid recollection is that of a discon-
certing incident when I spoke myself, on Lapsley's amendment. I had taken a seat near the Master, so as to be heard
more easily, and was next but one to Jackson. After I had got
through a sentence or so, Jackson rose, and I gave way,
thinking that he was interrupting me, or wished to raise a
point of order. But actually he was unaware that I was
speaking (he was very shortsighted and deaf), and proceeded
to make a quite long speech himself. The Master sensibly let
him have his way, and I was listened to very politely after he
had finished.

Jackson, as Vice-Master, was an *ex-officio* member of
Council, and his influence in the College, and particularly
among the senior Fellows, was still considerable, if not what
it had been twenty years before. It is therefore important to
realize that (with the possible exception of McTaggart) he
was the member of Council who held the most vehement views
about the war,† views which he stated on this occasion with
even more than his usual emphasis. My own recollection is

---

* I have often longed to move 'that the question "that the question be not
put" be not put', and wondered whether any chairman would accept such a
motion.

† See Parry's memoir of Jackson, pp. 93–113, especially p. 99, top.

24

that he began 'I am an old man, and I hope that the war may continue many years after my death'; but, though my recollection is as vivid and precise as any such recollection can be, I can get no definite confirmation from anyone else who was present.* The sentence, of course, is a good deal less 'shocking' than it sounds. 'Military victory is a long way off, and I do not expect to live to see it near: better that the war should continue for many years after I am dead than that it should be cut short by premature peace.' That would have been just what everybody would have expected from Jackson; but he was a very uncompromising person, afraid of nobody, and it would have been quite characteristic of him to prefer to express himself in an abrupt and startling way.

The resolution of the Council was never rescinded, and I suppose that it is still technically in force. The whole question seemed insignificant after the Russell case.

8. *Russell's position in the College before 1916*

I come now to the Russell case itself; and I must begin by explaining Russell's position in the College and how he came to hold it. This is one of the points in the case about which there has been most misunderstanding, and the misundertanding has been deepened by a statement made by Russell himself.

Russell was elected to a Fellowship in October 1895. This was one of the old 'Prize Fellowships', lasting six years and tenable without any obligation either of residence or of research.† He vacated his Fellowship in 1901.

* There was a certain amount of confusion, since two people were trying to speak. I was close to Jackson, and listening intently to every word (naturally, since, if it was an 'interruption', I should have had to reply to it at once).

† Under 'Title (α)' of the old statutes (X, XI, XII). Russell's dissertation formed the basis of his *An Essay on the Foundations of Geometry* (Cambridge University Press, 1897), now out of print.

In May 1910 he was appointed by the Council to a Lectureship in Logic and the Principles of Mathematics, tenable for five years from October 1910. The obligations of the lectureship were residence during full term and the delivery of one course of lectures per term, and the stipend was £210. It was not an ordinary appointment on the staff, carrying a Fellowship with it, but a special lectureship created as an encouragement to research and a contribution to University teaching.

Except for the Easter Term of 1914, when he was on leave of absence at Harvard, Russell lectured regularly up to the war. I have never heard it suggested that he was dissatisfied with the terms of his appointment. He wanted a definite academic position, but preferred one with light obligations which would leave him free for research.

By 1914, however, it was beginning to be felt (more, I think, by others than by Russell himself) that his position in the College was rather anomalous, and that a man of such distinction, living and lecturing regularly in College, ought to be a Fellow. This was represented to the Council, with special force, I believe, by Barnes; and on 12 February 1915 it was agreed that

> the Council is prepared to elect Mr Russell to a Fellowship under Title (ζ)* as soon as his lectureship is vacated by the effluxion of time or otherwise

(as would happen in October 1915). It should be observed that, although feeling here had not yet risen to any great height, there were already strong differences of opinion about the war, and Russell's attitude towards it was quite well known both in Cambridge and outside. This was not enough

---

* For Title (ζ) see the old statutes, X 5 a and XV 4 a. A Fellow elected under this title had 'to be engaged in the systematic pursuit of some important branch of University studies' and 'to have made or be likely to make valuable contributions to it'. He was bound to reside, and to lecture during one term of each year if the Council desired it.

to deter the Council from a course upon which they had no doubt already agreed in principle.

Feeling, however, was rising rapidly, and came to a head when, in May 1915, Russell applied for leave of absence for the following Michaelmas and Lent Terms. These would have been the first two terms of his tenure of his Fellowship. It was known that he proposed to occupy them in 'political' activity, and it is not surprising that there should have been strong opposition to his application. What followed is best described in the language of the Council Minutes.

21 May 1915

(i) It was agreed That, in electing to a Fellowship under Title (ζ), the Council should place on record a statement of the branch of studies in respect of the pursuit whereof the election was made.

(ii) It was agreed by 10 votes to 2 That the Council will in general be prepared to grant leave of absence to a Fellow elected under Title (ζ) only either on the ground of ill-health or urgent private affairs or on their being satisfied that the non-residence applied for is for the purpose of the better prosecution of research in the branch of studies in respect whereof he was elected. The Master, the Vice-Master, Dr Stanton, Mr Ball, Mr Parry, Dr McTaggart, Mr Whetham, Mr Innes, Mr Laurence, and Mr Dykes voted for the motion, Dr Barnes and Mr Winstanley voted against.

A letter from Mr Russell was read. It was agreed by 9 votes to 2 That Mr Russell be informed that should the Council elect him to a Fellowship under Title (ζ) it would be in view of his being engaged in the systematic study of Philosophy and Mathematics, and they would understand his acceptance of the Fellowship to indicate his intention to continue to devote himself to these studies. They would consider favourably an application for leave of non-residence if he informs them that the purpose of the application is the better prosecution of those studies. The Master, the Vice-Master, Mr Ball, Dr Parry, Dr McTaggart, Mr Whetham, Mr Innes, Mr Laurence and Mr Dykes voted for the motion, Dr Barnes and Mr Winstanley voted against.*

* Stanton abstaining.

28 May 1915

Two letters from Mr Russell were read. It was agreed That in agreement with Mr Russell's suggestion he be not elected to a Fellowship under Title (ζ), but that his lectureship be continued for five years from 1 October 1915 on the terms stated in Minute 6 of 27 May 1910, and that he be granted leave of absence for the Michaelmas Term 1915 and the Lent Term 1916.*

It will be seen that up to this point the relations between Russell and the Council were, on the surface at any rate, tolerably friendly. I was not on the Council, and have no direct knowledge of what was said at the meetings; and I have never been in the confidence of any member of the majority, so that I can only conjecture what their real feelings were. There must have been a considerable difference between the views actually expressed and the feelings which underlay them; for I am told that Russell's political opinions, which everybody knew to be the real source of trouble, were never mentioned throughout the discussions.

It is not necessarily illogical to grant leave of absence to a lecturer while denying it to a Fellow elected under Title (ζ), since a lecturer would normally receive no stipend when he was not actually discharging his duties,† while a Fellow must receive his modulus. And if I had been a member of the Council, had voted against Russell, and were anxious now to justify my vote, I suppose that this is the line of defence that I should follow. 'A Fellowship under Title (ζ) is given for the encouragement of research: it would be an abuse of a Fellowship, and a waste of College funds, to give one to a man who avows that he intends to occupy himself in an entirely different manner.' This is indeed

* Later (10 May 1916) he was given additional leave for the Lent and Easter Terms of 1917 in order to lecture at Harvard. Before then, of course, he had been dismissed.
† Unless on sabbatical or sick leave.

the point of view suggested by the Council's resolutions of 21 May.*

Was this really what was at the back of the minds of the Council? They would then, presumably, have passed the same resolutions whatever views Russell had professed about the war. Would they have acted in the same way if he had been ardently patriotic, and had proposed to spend a year making recruiting speeches? I can only say that I do not believe it.

As I said, I can only conjecture: but the Council knew quite well what Russell's opinions were, and my own belief is that their feelings were roughly as follows. 'We dislike Russell's views intensely. He intends to spend most of next year advocating them in public, and we feel sure that the public will begin to associate them with the College. This may not do much harm while he is only a lecturer, and we do not wish to provoke him into resigning his lectureship or refusing its prolongation, to which we are in any case almost committed. His election to a Fellowship (which must be announced in the press) would be much more disastrous, since it would be interpreted as a public gesture of approbation, and might have really serious effects on the future of the College. We will therefore not make him a Fellow; but we do not want to go out of our way to look for trouble, and we will let him have his way if he is prepared to remain in his present position.' I do not sympathize with this view, and would have voted with the minority if I had been a member of the Council; but I can understand it. It is substantially the view expressed by Lapsley, in another context, at the College Meeting about the U.D.C.

It is very unfortunate that Russell's one allusion to all these

* There was one possible course which, rather oddly, does not seem to have been suggested either by any member of the Council or by Russell himself: viz. that the election should be deferred until the end of the war, the Council undertaking to elect Russell then if College finances allowed it.

controversies in his writings should be so misleading. He writes:*

I was invited by Trinity College, Cambridge, to become a lecturer, but not a Fellow. The difference is not pecuniary; it is that a Fellow has a voice in the government of the College, and cannot be dispossessed during the term of his Fellowship except for grave immorality. The reason for not offering me a Fellowship was that the clerical party did not wish to add to the anti-clerical vote. The result was that they were able to dismiss me in 1916, when they disliked my views on the war....

This passage suggests a good many comments.

(1) The College, as distinct from the Council, had no say in the matter at any stage, until the final memorial to the Council, after the war, which led to Russell's reinstatement; and Russell, writing for a public which knows nothing of the constitution of Trinity, should, in fairness to the College, have made this clear.†

(2) There is always something in a large society like Trinity which, though actually it will include very few clergymen, can be described by a stretch of language as the 'clerical party'. There is a 'religious' and an 'irreligious' party, though the boundary between them is shifting and ill-defined; and there is no doubt that the 'religious' party included men who disliked Russell, and whose dislike of him, before 1914, was primarily inspired by his 'infidelity'. But the feeling against him after 1914 was almost entirely political, and there was no sort of correlation between 'political' and 'religious' dislike. We need only look at the divisions which I have just quoted from the Council Minutes: the two members of the

* *Sceptical Essays* (1928), p. 150.

† I may seem to be laying too much stress on a minor point, since the Council is an executive body appointed by the College. But (as I explained on p. 8) the relations between the College and the Council in 1916 were quite abnormal, and there was no effective check on any of the Council's actions. Russell would certainly never have been dismissed if the decision had depended on a majority of the whole society.

Council who stood by Russell throughout, namely Barnes and Winstanley, must plainly both be classified (if we are to make such a classification) as members of the 'religious' party.*

It must also be remembered that, even if there had been a 'clerical party' anxious to frustrate Russell, it would certainly not have been in a position to carry the College with it. There had been one 'religious' controversy in the College a little before, when the Council, in 1912, had attempted to restore compulsory chapel. In this the 'clerical party' had been decisively defeated, and the opposition had been led by the very men (Jackson and McTaggart) who were Russell's most bitter opponents later.

9. *The Everett leaflet*

On 10 April 1916 Ernest F. Everett, a conscientious objector, was sentenced to two years' hard labour, for disobedience to military orders, by a district court-martial at Abergele.

There was nothing to distinguish his case from that of many other conscientious objectors. Everett had been a school-master at St Helens, and was a member of the N.C.F. He appeared before the local and appeal tribunals, 'both of which treated him very unfairly, going out of their way to recommend his dismissal from school'.† He was granted exemption from combatant service.

His actions later were typical of those of many others of the most honest objectors. He took no notice when called up, and

* There were four clergymen on the Council, the Master, Stanton, Parry, and Barnes. Barnes was Russell's most vehement supporter, and Stanton (though he voted later for Russell's expulsion) had abstained in the critical division of 21 May. Barnes left Cambridge before the question of expulsion arose.

† I quote from the leaflet, as Mr Bodkin did at the Mansion House. I have not seen any report of the proceedings before the tribunals, and have no reason for supposing that these particular tribunals were notably better or worse than most. No doubt Everett might have fared better in Cambridge.

There is a copy of the leaflet in the University Library.

on 31 March he was arrested as an absentee, brought before the magistrates, fined £2, and handed over to the military authorities. He was then taken to Warrington Barracks, where he was compelled to put on uniform; and on the next day he was moved to Abergele and placed in the Non-Combatant Corps.

Here (like others who found themselves in his position) he adopted a consistent policy of passive resistance to all military orders. It is not suggested that he was truculent, or, on the other hand, that he was bullied.* 'The Corporal, the Lieutenant, the Captain, and the Colonel' all seem to have dealt with him 'in quite a considerate way'.† In short, up to the time of the inevitable court-martial, everybody seems to have behaved quite well.

The sentence of two years' hard labour was that habitually passed by courts-martial in similar cases: we need not suppose that this court was exceptionally ferocious. It may seem a savage sentence to pass on an admittedly honest man, and I hardly suppose that anybody would attempt to justify it now. But it is improbable that Everett's court-martial, or many of the other courts-martial which passed similar sentences, imagined that they were likely to be served in full.‡ In fact Everett's sentence was commuted, to 112 days' detention, within three weeks, as soon as the facts about the case became widely known.

The leaflet which was the ground for Russell's prosecution was issued by the N.C.F. on 19 April. It was written by Russell, except for one paragraph (which I shall quote in a moment, and for which he accepted responsibility); but there is nothing in it in the least characteristic of Russell's style. It is quite short, and most of its two pages are occupied by a bald

---

* A good many conscientious objectors were treated rather brutally by N.C.O.'s.

† I quote Mr Bodkin, and have no reason for doubting him.

‡ I believe that there were a few cases of imprisonment for the full period, some of which had disastrous results.

narrative of the undisputed facts of the case. This is followed by a paragraph printed in heavy type (and actually added at the headquarters of the N.C.F.).

> The sentence was two years hard labour. Everett is now suffering this savage punishment solely for refusal to go against his conscience. He is fighting the old fight for liberty, and against religious persecution, in the same spirit in which martyrs suffered in the past. Will you join the persecutors? Or will you stand for those who are defending conscience at the cost of obloquy and pain of mind and body?
>
> Forty other men are suffering persecution for conscience sake in the same way as Mr Everett. Can you remain silent while this goes on?

It was on this paragraph that the prosecution mainly relied. The Archbishop of Canterbury said much the same, in more cautious language, in speeches in the House of Lords and letters to ministers.

I find it hard to believe that the Government, if left to themselves, would have troubled about the leaflet, but their hands, and Russell's, were forced by the action of local authorities in Liverpool and elsewhere. A number of men were arrested and imprisoned for distributing the leaflet, and it was impossible for Russell to remain silent when he heard of this. He therefore wrote a letter to *The Times* which appeared on 17 May 1916.

Adsum qui feci

Sir

> A leaflet was lately issued by the No Conscription Fellowship dealing with the case of Mr Everett, a conscientious objector who was sentenced to two years hard labour by court-martial for disobedience to the military authorities. Six men have been condemned to varying terms of imprisonment with hard labour for distributing this leaflet. I wish to make it known that I am the author of this leaflet, and that, if anyone is to be prosecuted, I am the person primarily responsible.
>
> Yours faithfully,
>
> BERTRAND RUSSELL

10. *Rex* v. *Bertrand Russell: the prosecution*

This letter, of course, made prosecution inevitable, and Russell appeared before the Lord Mayor (Sir Charles Wakefield) at the Mansion House on 5 June 1916. Mr A. H. Bodkin (later Sir Archibald Bodkin, and Director of Public Prosecutions from 1920 to 1930) appeared for the prosecution;* Russell defended himself. The charge was that of making, in a printed publication, 'statements likely to prejudice the recruiting and discipline of His Majesty's forces'. A verbatim report of the case was published by the N.C.F., but suppressed almost immediately. I have a copy, and there is one in the University Library.†

Mr Bodkin's speech was both unfair and feeble, and it seems a pity now that the Crown could not brief a better counsel. His case was not a strong one; and he made it still weaker, quite unnecessarily, by laying all his emphasis on *recruiting*. 'The sole questions are: did the Defendant make any statement in such a manner: secondly, was that statement of a character likely to prejudice recruiting?' Of *discipline* he says nothing at all: it was left to Russell himself to suggest that a case, not indeed strong, but at any rate more plausible, might have been stated on that ground.

Mr Bodkin began by reciting the admitted facts, that Everett had disobeyed orders and had been sentenced to two years' hard labour, that the leaflet was a protest against the severity of the sentence,‡ and that Russell had admitted its authorship. There is nothing in all this which calls for comment except a very unworthy attempt to excite prejudice against Russell by a suggestion that he had tried to shirk the consequences of his action.

---

* He also appeared in the Morel case in September 1917.
† There is also a summary of the proceedings in *The Cambridge Review* for 1 March 1940.
‡ He did not mention, naturally, that it had already been commuted.

But whilst, as appearing for the prosecution, one is bound to use moderate language, the position of those other six persons who had been dealt with for distributing this leaflet gives food for considerable thought. It was not until six of them had been dealt with by different courts of summary jurisdiction in different parts of the country that Mr Bertrand Russell accepted responsibility.

Everett was sentenced on 10 April, the leaflet began to be distributed about 19 or 20 April, the six men were prosecuted on different dates 'in different parts of the country', with the right of appeal, and Russell's letter appeared in the *Times* on 17 May. The suggestion is monstrous, has never been made by anyone else, and would never have been made by a first-rate counsel.

In justification of his main thesis, that the leaflet was likely to 'prejudice recruiting', Mr Bodkin really said nothing at all; he seems to have assumed (as it proved correctly) that a little appeal to the passions of the moment was all that was wanted.

Our submission is that...coming from this organization which is supporting those who find that their consciences permit them to take advantage of the security of the country, but refuse to permit them to do anything which tends to secure the security of the country, that it has the tendency of preventing recruiting for that reason....

One thing which is perfectly certain about it is that there is not a syllable in it from beginning to end which is likely to assist recruiting....

And stern views must be taken if you find that refusal to obey orders, and mutinous and insubordinate conduct, is not that of a mere isolated individual, but is the conduct of a person who is acting in combination with others, or with many others—it is necessary to deal differently with persons under different circumstances, whether they are acting entirely alone as individuals, or whether, as I say, in combination with, or supported by others, or by organizations which live by the support that they can apparently give to those who find that their consciences do not permit them to obey the law of the country.

A verbatim report is cruel to an indifferent speaker; but Mr Bodkin's oratory was worse than his law.

11. *Rex* v. *Bertrand Russell: the defence*

Russell's speech in defence is naturally much abler and more interesting. It is rather too long, and some of his argument near the end was ruled out by the Lord Mayor as irrelevant: it was a handicap to him that Mr Bodkin had not really stated any case for him to answer, so that he had to construct one himself. Thus the last part of the speech reads like that of a man who knows that he has prepared too much and is trying to compress his notes rather hastily. There is also an occasional touch of the epigrammatic quality which so infuriated all Russell's opponents. But on the whole it is excellent, well argued, well expressed, and remarkably good-tempered.

He begins with a general discussion of the nature of the charge: he had to explain it somehow, and Mr Bodkin had given him very little help. Russell tries to elucidate it by quotations from Mr Herbert Samuel (now Viscount Samuel, then Home Secretary). 'It is one thing to advocate repeal of the compulsory Military Service Act. It is another thing to advocate resistance to its provisions.' 'Advocacy of resistance', then, is an offence. What, Russell asks, is considered to be 'advocacy of resistance'? Mr Bodkin had not used the phrase, but I do not think that Russell's discussion is in any way irrelevant, since it seems plain that 'advocacy of resistance', in some sense never clearly defined, was the kernel of the charge.

What, then, is 'advocating resistance'?

> Is a conscientious objector advocating resistance if he says 'I intend not to perform military service, even if the tribunals should fail to grant me exemption'? Or if, having failed to obtain exemption, he states that he as a conscientious objector cannot conform to that decision? Is he in saying that advocating resistance? I do not think that that view can be held. . . .
> A conscientious objection is by its very nature one which

cannot be overridden by any decision of the Court of Law . . .
therefore it cannot be said that a man is advocating resistance
. . . by a mere statement that he himself does not propose to
perform military service, even if he should fail to obtain
exemption. I think some such statement he is bound to make
by law when he comes before the tribunals, because if he
were willing to obey the decision he would not be a genuine
objector, and would not be entitled to the exemption of the
Act. . . .

Next,

If a man has a right to state that he himself cannot obey
the law under certain contingencies, and that right is accorded
by the conscience clause, it cannot surely be against the law
to state on behalf of other people that there are such men. . . .
It cannot be construed as advocacy of resistance to state what
is, after all, a patent fact, that resistance is occurring, and
will continue so long as the present system is persisted in.

Mr Samuel had said himself in the House of Commons—

I can understand the individual conscientious objector
saying as an individual 'Whatever happens to me I do not
care. I hold certain doctrines, and no human power can ever
compel me to form part of a military organization.' . . . Such
a man can be respected. . . .

But, says Russell, that

is the very thing which I said in this leaflet, in effect the same
sentiments. That is the gist of this pamphlet—merely adding
the particular circumstances and particular facts.

All this argument seems to me quite relevant and essentially
sound. Indeed it seems to me plain that, if 'advocacy of
resistance' was the real ground of offence, then the Government were prosecuting the wrong man. The real offenders
were, not of course Everett, in doing his duty according to his
lights, nor Russell, in protesting against Everett's sentence,
but the leaders of the N.C.F. *They*, unquestionably, had
'advocated resistance'—it was the avowed object, for example, of Clifford Allen's address;* and in doing so they had

* See pp. 15–16.

37

perhaps given reasonable ground for prosecution. Even so their offence would have lain, not in their activities in connection with this particular case, but in their very existence as an organization.

On the main charge (as defined by Mr Bodkin) Russell is almost too effective.

> I do not think that there is any evidence possible to adduce, and no evidence has been adduced, in favour of the view that this leaflet prejudices recruiting. At the time when it was issued, single men were already subject to conscription, and therefore any supposed effect would have been only in regard to married men. Now, the married man who contemplates voluntarily enlisting is *ex hypothesi* not a conscientious objector. The leaflet informs him that if he chooses to pose as a conscientious objector he is liable to two years' hard labour. I do not consider that knowledge of that fact is likely to induce such a man to pretend that he is a conscientious objector when he is not.

It is sound enough argument, but put in a way more likely to appeal to Fellows of Trinity than to Lord Mayors with inelastic minds.*

A little later Russell refers to the particular sentence 'Will you join the persecutors?' which occurs in the last paragraph of the leaflet. It had been suggested (to do him justice, not by Mr Bodkin) that this meant 'Will you join the Army?', and was therefore a direct incitement against recruiting. Russell had naturally no difficulty in showing the absurdity of this suggestion.

> I do not think it is the meaning which any reader is likely to attach to it....I do not consider that the Army are the persecutors. The Army authorities are merely carrying

---

* Russell may seem to be setting up a dummy in order to knock it down. Here again he suffers from Mr Bodkin's incoherency: he has to state the case against himself somehow, and it is not easy to think of much more plausible arguments. 'Courts-martial are apt to pass ferocious sentences on virtuous people; it is unlikely that conscientious objectors alone will suffer; to make an outcry about the sentences will make men hesitate who would otherwise be willing to join, and will therefore discourage recruiting': this seems to me about equally feeble.

out the law.... The persecutors are the Government and their supporters; the tribunals...; the Press...; and that large body of public opinion which has allowed hatred and contempt to blind it to inhumanity and injustice. 'Will you join the persecutors?' means 'Will you join this section of the public?'...

Next Russell passes to the question whether the leaflet was likely to prejudice *discipline* (which Mr Bodkin had ignored).

The purpose of the leaflet is to make it known that a man is liable to two years' hard labour for refusing to obey discipline. Does this encourage a man to resist discipline?

If the authorities... were right in inflicting the sentences—right from the point of view of promoting discipline—they must be wrong in saying that the leaflet is prejudicial to discipline in making them known. We know that when a court-martial sentence is pronounced steps are taken to promulgate it publicly in the camp or barracks, to make the soldiers know what sentences have been pronounced....

I do not know whether the prosecution would suggest that conscientious objectors are stimulated to resistance by the knowledge of what their comrades are suffering. That, perhaps, may have an element of truth in it, but if so that is not a motive that would appeal to a shirker....

It is true that this leaflet does not confine itself to a mere statement of facts. There is in the last paragraph a criticism of these facts. It may be said that discipline is endangered by this phrase: 'Everett is now suffering this savage punishment for refusing to go against his conscience.'... I would point out that that sentence is one which might appear specially prejudicial to discipline, but, I would ask you, is all criticism of a court-martial sentence to be held illegal? We know that practically every time a woman is condemned to be hanged for murder there is a petition for a commutation of her sentence. This is certainly legal. Are court-martial sentences in a different position?...

He then cites the case of the conscientious objectors at that time in France, and legally liable to be shot. Suppose that they were—'there would be a storm of protest from Bishops, from eminent nonconformists, from Members of Parliament.... Would these protests be illegal?'

39

I hardly think that I need quote more of Russell's speech (the last part of which does not in any case seem to me so good). I will merely state my own conclusions about the merits of the case.

The Government knew quite well that the sentence on Everett was indefensible, and admitted this when they decided to commute it. Russell's leaflet was the cause of this decision. They had no desire to prosecute the distributors of the pamphlet, and still less to prosecute Russell; but their hands were forced, first by the action of local police authorities, then by Russell's challenge. It was essential to them that the prosecution, once begun, should be successful, and they should therefore have entrusted it to an abler advocate than Mr Bodkin; for the case, weak as it was, could at any rate have been much better presented. It is arguable that the decision to prosecute was justified politically, that Russell was a dangerous man and that it was necessary to do something to check him; but it is not seriously arguable that he was guilty of the offence of which he was convicted. The Government virtually admitted this also when they suppressed the report of the case.

12. *Russell's dismissal*

Russell was found guilty and fined £100 (with £10 costs and the alternative of 61 days' imprisonment). The sentence was confirmed on appeal.* He declined to pay the fine, but, since he had valuable books in his rooms which could be seized and sold, there was never any question of his going to prison. The books were however saved by the action of his friends, who subscribed the necessary £100 and offered that sum for the first book put up at the auction.

* The appeal was heard before the City Quarter Sessions, at the Guildhall, on 29 June 1916. There is no full account of the proceedings, which were less interesting than those at the Mansion House.

The College Council met on 11 July 1916, when

> It was agreed unanimously that, since Mr. Russell has been convicted under the Defence of the Realm Act, and his conviction has been confirmed on appeal, he be removed from his lectureship in the College.

The members present were the Master, the Vice-Master, Stanton, Ball, Parry, Duff, McTaggart, Whetham, Innes, Laurence, and Dykes. Barnes and Winstanley, who had supported Russell before, had left Cambridge, the former permanently, the latter on war service in Egypt.

The action of the Council at once aroused a storm of protest. The letter from Innes informing Russell of the decision was printed in the *Cambridge Magazine* of 14 October 1916, and accompanied by an article 'Trinity in Disgrace— America's Opportunity'* and by a number of interesting extracts from letters.

Thus D. S. Robertson, writing from France as 'a Fellow and Lecturer of Trinity absent on military service',† said

> The Court found that Mr Russell's action was illegal; but the Council of Trinity were free to judge whether or not it was dishonourable. Their refusal to draw such a distinction seems to me an inexpressible disaster to tolerance and liberty.

Mr Hilton Young (now Lord Kennet), in a letter dated from H.M.S. *Centaur*, wrote

> What brings me here? The desire that England should remain, and that Europe should become, a place in which the Russells whom fate grants us from time to time should be free to stimulate and annoy us unpersecuted.... That Trinity should gratuitously number itself among the persecutors, this is more discouraging than a German victory.

The *Magazine* also quotes from a letter of Professor Gilbert Murray in *The Nation*—'my first impression on hearing of the

---

* Russell was invited to Harvard, but the Foreign Office refused him a passport.
† His letter appeared first in the *Nation* on 16 Sept. 1916.

41

course the Council had taken was to treat the story as incredible'.

A memorial was sent to the Council a little later signed by 22 Fellows.

Private and confidential

The undersigned Fellows of the College, while not proposing to take any action in the matter during the war, desire to place it on record that they are not satisfied with the action of the College in depriving Mr Russell of his lectureship.

James Ward	J. E. Littlewood	C. N. S. Woolf
A. N. Whitehead[1]	H. A. Hollond	F. R. Tennant
E. W. Barnes	D. S. Robertson	J. R. M. Butler
F. M. Cornford	F. A. Simpson	Sydney Chapman
E. Harrison	A. Gow	E. D. Adrian
G. H. Hardy	Eric H. Neville	Ralph H. Fowler
Denys A. Winstanley	C. D. Broad	J. Proudman
A. S. Eddington		

[1] Unless the Council proposes to offer to Mr Russell a suitable academic post.

I have no idea what Whitehead was thinking of in his reservation.

The protest was a feeble one, as protests signed by any considerable number of people are apt to be. It was essential to get as many signatures as we could, and as quickly as possible. Many likely signatories were away; communication with them was slow and uncertain*; and it was difficult to be sure what the reactions of some of them might be. Stronger language might well have resulted in refusals to sign.

It was also certain that no protest was in the least likely to produce any immediate result. We could, of course, have summoned a College Meeting and moved a direct vote of censure; but, even if it had proved possible to persuade most of our supporters to such drastic action, a good many of them would have been unable to attend, and we should certainly have been beaten, as we had been beaten at the meeting

* Thus we could not get D. H. Robertson's signature.

about the U.D.C. The Council, in fact, were for the time in an impregnable position; they had only to sit tight and say nothing. It must be remembered that they were firmly convinced, in spite of a good deal of evidence to the contrary, that their action would be applauded by the great majority of the absent Fellows when they returned. In fact they believed this right up to 1919.

Still less, of course, were the Council likely to pay any attention to outside criticism. In the circumstances there was nothing to be done but to put *some* protest on record, signed by as many Fellows as possible, and wait for the end of the war.

13. *Reflections on the action of the Council*

It was never questioned that the Council, when they dismissed Russell, were acting within their legal rights. A lecturer held office 'during the pleasure of the Council',* and could, in theory at any rate, be dismissed for any reason or none: the general body of Fellows had no direct say in the matter. It would have been possible (though quite useless) to challenge the legality of the action of the Council about the U.D.C., but in this case it was indisputable.

It is also clear that the Council were bound to take notice of Russell's conviction, and to consider whether any action on their part was called for. This is shown conclusively by the statutes concerning 'Power of Removal of Fellows'. Russell was not a Fellow, but any reason sufficient for the removal of a Fellow would be a still more sufficient reason for the dismissal of a lecturer who was not a Fellow.

Statute XVII (of the old statutes) states three sets of circumstances in which the Council 'may' or 'shall' consider the removal of a Fellow.

* Statute XXXIV. 2. In the new statutes (XXXIV. 3) 'pleasure' has been changed to 'satisfaction'.

1. If any Fellow shall be convicted by a court of competent jurisdiction of a crime of whatever nature or description, the Master shall with all convenient speed assemble a meeting of the Council exclusive of such Fellow if a member of Council. The Council so assembled may if they think fit proceed to inquire into the case, and, if the fact of such conviction be established, may, by a resolution in which the votes of seven members of Council (the Master being one) shall concur, expel such Fellow from the College.

2. If any three Fellows of the College or any two members of the Council shall prefer before the Master against any Fellow a charge of disgraceful conduct, the Master shall... (act as under 1).

3. If the Master shall in any case think it proper to cause an inquiry to be instituted as to whether or not the conduct of any Fellow has been disgraceful, he may... (act as under 1).

In the new statutes Clause 1 has been removed, but I have no reason for supposing that the College had the Russell case in mind when they made this change.

In view of these provisions, the Council were bound to consider the case. It is true that Clause 1 is not compulsory (except on the Master): the Council 'may if they think fit proceed to inquire...'. But it would have been very surprising if they had not 'proceeded to inquire'; and it is certain that, with feeling what it was, some two members of Council, or the Master himself, would have forced action under Clause 2 or Clause 3 even if the majority had been unwilling to act under Clause 1. In any case nobody has denied that they were justified in instituting an inquiry.

The actual resolution of the Council would imply, if it were to be interpreted quite literally, that any lecturer found guilty of an offence under the Defence of the Realm Act should be dismissed, without regard either to the importance or the merits of his case, and without any opportunity of being heard in his own defence. Such an interpretation would have been preposterous even in 1916, since the offence might have been a trivial and unintentional breach of the black-out regulations. It is obvious that in such a case the Council must consider whether the offence is serious; and we may assume that they did so in this case, and satisfied themselves that 'making statements likely to prejudice the recruiting and discipline of His Majesty's forces' was a really serious offence (as of course it well might be). In this they might reasonably be guided by the publicity of the case, the importance which the military authorities seemed to attach to it, and the magnitude of the fine or other penalty inflicted. The questions which remain are: first, whether it was their duty to form an independent judgement of the justice of the conviction; secondly, whether in fact they tried to do so.

It is obvious that only a member of the Council can answer the second question, but my own belief is that they did not. I cannot produce real 'evidence' in support of this belief, and none of the letters which I have been shown, and from which I shall quote later, throw any light upon the question. But it seems incredible to me that the Council, if they really wanted to satisfy themselves that Russell had been convicted justly, should not have asked him, or his friends, for his defence. This, I am sure, they never did: I do not believe that any member of Council ever even read the verbatim report of the proceedings.

In this case the Council must have answered the first question negatively. They would have said, I suppose, that it was not their business to retry the case; that Russell had been convicted by a 'competent court' with all the facts before it, and that they could not consider whether there had been a miscarriage of justice, but must accept the verdict as final. I do not suggest that this attitude is altogether indefensible; it might be the attitude of the Law Society, or the General Medical Council, in the case of a solicitor convicted of fraud, or a doctor of adultery with one of his patients.

The important question is not whether the Council could put up a sound technical defence of their action, but whether

45

it was sensible, and likely to promote the real interests of the College. And naturally I find it impossible to answer this question in their favour; I condemned their action at the time, and I condemn it still after twenty-five years' reflection. Whatever they may have thought, there were so many reasons for hesitation. They should have remembered that pacifists, and especially provocative pacifists like Russell, are most unlikely to get fair play in time of war, that many of them had already been convicted very unjustly, and that the justice of the conviction of any pacifist was suspect. They should also have remembered that the public opinion of which they were so frightened was unbalanced and hysterical, and that its currents were quite likely to reverse themselves as soon as the war was over. Above all they should have remembered that Fellows of Trinity are people whose reactions are often a little difficult to forecast; that they might be mistaken in their judgement of the opinions of absent Fellows; that their action was certain to be challenged when the absent Fellows returned; and that they might then find themselves in a position from which they could escape only by a rather humiliating withdrawal. I do not accuse any member of the Council of malice or vindictiveness: their failure was a failure of imagination and common sense.

14. *The second Russell case*

Russell was prosecuted for the second time on 11 February 1918, for 'having in a printed publication made certain statements likely to prejudice His Majesty's relations with the United States of America'. The statements in question had appeared in an article in *The Tribunal* entitled 'The German Peace Offer', and the sentence which was picked out as particularly objectionable ran

> The American garrison which will by that time be occupying England and France, whether or not they will prove

46

efficient against the Germans, will no doubt be capable of intimidating strikers, an occupation to which the American Army is accustomed at home.

It is of course a foolish and reckless sentence, the kind of sentence which an able man could write only after a long course of exasperation. Russell had written a good many provocative articles in the *Tribunal* and elsewhere, and it is quite likely that by now the Government wanted to prosecute him. He could not have given them a better opportunity, since it was in America that his reputation was highest, and this was just the thing to alienate American sympathy.

The case was heard by Sir John Dickinson at Bow Street, Mr Travers Humphreys prosecuting and Mr Cecil Whiteley defending. The decision to prosecute may or may not have been wise, but this time there was no doubt that Russell was guilty. He was sentenced to six months' imprisonment in the second division. This was varied to the first division on appeal to the London Sessions on 2 May 1918, the Chairman (Mr Lawrie) justifying his decision on the ground that 'it would be a great loss to the country if Mr Russell, a man of great distinction, were confined in such a manner that his abilities did not have full scope'. He was much luckier than Morel, whose health was badly broken by imprisonment.* Actually he did not suffer seriously, and wrote his *Introduction to Mathematical Philosophy* in Brixton Prison.

It is important that the facts about this second conviction should be stated explicitly, because of the widespread misapprehension which I mentioned at the beginning,† but it had no direct effect on Russell's relations with Trinity: he was not, at the time, even a member of the College.‡ It was of course a blow to his supporters, since it seemed likely to make his reinstatement after the war a good deal more difficult. Actually, it made surprisingly little difference. Ward, one of

---

* See Lord Snowden's *Autobiography*, vol. I, p. 424.   † See p. 1.
‡ He had taken his name off the books after his dismissal.

his staunchest supporters, said afterwards that he would have regarded dismissal on *this* ground as justifiable;* and no doubt the second conviction stiffened the obstinacy of the Council. But none of his supporters went back on him, and I do not believe that the Council would have reinstated him voluntarily in any case.

15. *The memorial for Russell's reinstatement*

It was always certain that there would be a demand for Russell's reinstatement when the war was over and the Fellows who had been absent on military service returned, but there was a good deal of difference of opinion about the best method of procedure. There was a minority which wanted definitely to censure the Council by resolution at a Special College Meeting,† but the great majority wished to be as conciliatory as possible, and to leave them the easiest road for retreat. There were even some who thought that the Council might anticipate the demand and reinstate Russell voluntarily, but it soon became obvious that there was no hope of this.

In these circumstances there was bound to be considerable delay, and it was not until near the end of 1919 that a memorial, in the form of a letter to the Master, was actually received by the Council. The letter had been drafted, and signatures collected, by Hollond.

From the Minutes of the Council

28 November 1919

A letter signed by 27 Fellows asking that Mr Russell be appointed to a lectureship was received and ordered to be circulated.

* See p. 52.
† This was Ward's view (see p. 53), and also my own. No doubt it was well that we were overruled.

(i) The Council had under consideration a letter signed by 28 Fellows and supported by 5 other Fellows asking that Mr Russell be invited to return to the College as a lecturer and pointing out that such an invitation would involve no implication that the action taken during the war was not right in the circumstances. It was agreed that the letter be placed in the Report Book.

(ii) It was agreed that a lectureship in Logic and the Principles of Mathematics tenable for five years from 1 July 1920 be offered to Mr Russell; that he be required to reside in Cambridge during full term and to deliver one course of lectures a term on the subjects of his lectureship; and that he receive a stipend of 250 guineas a year payable from the general corporate revenue, together with rooms in College to be held under the conditions applying to Fellows in Class B, and dinner in Hall.

The members of Council present on 12 December were the Master (J. J. Thomson), the Vice-Master (Parry), Stanton, Herman, McTaggart, Whetham, Innes, Harrison, Laurence, Lapsley, and Hollond. Whetham left before (ii). Thomson had been appointed Master in 1918, and Parry had succeeded Jackson as Vice-Master in 1919. The Master, Herman, Harrison, Lapsley and Hollond had not been on the Council in 1916.

From the Report Book

Dear Master,

Those of the Fellows of the College whose names are appended to this letter wish to express strongly their hope that Mr Russell may be appointed to a lectureship, and respectfully request that you will communicate this letter to the Council.

It seems to us that it is possible for those who approved the action taken by the Council during the war, in depriving Mr Russell of his lectureship, to consider without inconsistency that the best interests of the College would now be served by an invitation being sent to him to return. Such an invitation would involve no implication that the action taken during the war was not right in the circumstances then obtaining, and indeed among the signatories of this letter are some who support that action.

There appear to us to be the following reasons why it is desirable that the proposal which we make should be carried into effect.

When the events of to-day come in the future to be viewed in perspective, failure to reinstate Mr Russell after the relaxing of war tension would, we think, be regarded, and rightly regarded, as unworthy of the intellectual traditions of our Society, and as indicative of the existence in it of a spirit of intolerance. All the more will this be so if Mr Russell attains, as there seems reason to believe that, with the diffusion of knowledge of his work, he will attain, a position of outstanding distinction in the history of science.

As regards the present, when it is known that a former Fellow of the College, whose intellectual achievements rank on a level with those of the most distinguished of its members, would prefer, from love of the Society, to serve the College in a poorly paid capacity rather than to accept a position elsewhere, we should feel humiliated if his willingness to undertake such service were to be ignored.

Further, we confidently hope that the granting of our request will promote the unity of the College. It is unavoidable, and even desirable, that there should exist in a Society like ours conflicts of opinion with regard to duties and values in life. But there have been times, especially under the stress of war, when such differences have produced tension in personal relations. We feel that at the conclusion of a war, which has inflicted on most members of our Society grievous mental suffering, a determined effort should be made to suppress all such antagonisms.

It is, and always has been, the sincere intention of every one of the signatories of this letter, in the event of this proposal being rejected, to preserve in the fullest possible way the amenities of social intercourse. But it is inevitable that the further exclusion from the College, in consequence of conduct for which he has already suffered heavily, of a former colleague for whom many Fellows have a warm affection, would produce a continuing soreness of feeling on their part, which would make the maintenance of harmony depend on conscious effort rather than on the spontaneous sympathy which membership of our Foundation should imply.

50

If on the other hand those members of the Council who are not *a priori* in agreement with the object of this letter can come to the conclusion that the interests of the College will be served by taking account of the strength of feeling existing with regard to this matter, we feel sure that there will be such an instinctive tightening of the bond of corporate feeling as will be of the happiest augury for the future of our Society. As for Mr Russell's own attitude, we know that he is ready to forget the past. There have been too many occasions during his career on which his sense of duty has compelled him to perform tasks that were disagreeable to him, for him not to recognize in others the consciousness of a similar obligation, and not to realize that to many members of the Council the duty of voting for the termination of his appointment must have been exceedingly painful. We know that he will feel no rancour against those members of the Council who took this course, and that he will welcome the resumption of social relations with them on the basis of mutual courtesy and toleration.

We feel that the question cannot be deferred longer. Mr Russell has reached an age at which it is desirable both on personal and on intellectual grounds that he should have a settled position; and it would be unfortunate if he were subjected to continued uncertainty regarding his future.

We are, Master, yours faithfully,

A. N. Whitehead	F. A. Simpson	O. D. Schreiner
F. M. Cornford	F. R. Tennant	E. Rutherford
E. Harrison	J. R. M. Butler	G. I. Taylor
G. H. Hardy	E. D. Adrian	T. C. Nicholas
D. A. Winstanley	R. H. Fowler	D. R. Pye
A. S. Eddington	D. H. Robertson	T. H. Marshall
J. E. Littlewood	N. K. Adam	E. A. Milne
H. A. Hollond	J. Burnaby	S. Pollard
D. S. Robertson	J. Proudman	R. R. Sedgwick

Buxton signed later. The letter was not sent to Ramanujan, who was ill in India and died soon after. Chapman and Bragg had been willing to sign, but ceased to be Fellows before the memorial was presented.* Ward, Langley, Fletcher,

* There were other signatories of the 1916 protest (Barnes, Gow, Neville, and Broad) who had ceased to be Fellows before the memorial was drafted, and were therefore not asked to sign. Woolf had been killed.

Hopkins, and Southwell preferred not to sign, but signified their support of the memorial in personal letters to the Master.

The memorial was signed or supported by an absolute majority of the Society, by every Fellow under 45 except Laurence, Dykes and Ramanujan, and by every Fellow who had served in the forces.*

The Scholars also sent in a memorial: I have not seen it, but I am told that it was signed by all but one of some fifty or sixty Scholars in residence.

16. Comments on the memorial

There were some of us who did not altogether like signing Hollond's letter. In particular we disliked the second paragraph, which seemed to us to carry 'conciliation' too far. There were not likely to be many signatories who thought the Council's action excusable, and we thought that we could, if necessary, secure Russell's reinstatement without them. It was a little hard for those of us who had been most outspoken in our condemnation to associate ourselves with such half-hearted supporters and speak now in so soft a tone. We seemed almost to be admitting that after all we might have been wrong.

This was why Ward preferred not to sign the letter; and my own feelings, though actually I signed, were much the same as his. In his letter to the Master signifying his support of the memorial he wrote 'I doubt if I shall ever be convinced that the first decision of the Council in this case was justifiable',† and in a letter to Hollond he expressed himself much more decidedly. This letter I quote in full.

* See Appendix A. Laurence and Dykes had both been members of the Council which dismissed Russell. Ramanujan would of course have signed.

† He went on to say 'I admit that such a decision following the second offence would have been', and here I could not have followed him, though I should of course have admitted that it would have been much more excusable.

Dear Hollond,

I do not, so far as I remember, object to anything said in your letter about Russell himself; but I am averse to saying anything that would whitewash the action of the Council in dismissing him as they did; nor do I think it wise to intimate that, if they do not reinstate him, they will be regarded as still animated by an intolerant spirit.

Personally I should have preferred to have a College Meeting put on record some form of censure of the past act of the Council, and at the same time urging that it should, so to say, be rescinded. But possibly the latter is beyond the powers of a College Meeting.

Also I am inclined to agree with Whitehead that the step you are taking should have been preceded by an informal discussion, at which all of us who are in favour of movement should have had an opportunity of stating their views.

However it is now too late for that, as doubtless the letter has received many signatories. But, as I said to Simpson, I am ready to support it by writing on my own account to the Master as soon as I know that the letter has been forwarded.

Yours sincerely,

JAMES WARD.

These were very much my own feelings (and in fact, throughout the whole controversy, I agreed with Ward more nearly than with anyone else). But I had to admit that the letter was well adapted for its purpose, that it made Russell's reinstatement almost certain, and that that was after all the essential thing. Accordingly I signed.

Of course there is a threat behind the mild language of the memorial. The Council are given every opportunity to retreat with the least possible loss of dignity, but if they do not retreat voluntarily they will be compelled to. The signatories command their majority and mean to have their way; and the Council must have recognized this at once. The Fellows as a whole have no voice in an appointment or a dismissal: direct interference in such a matter is, as Ward says, beyond the powers of a College Meeting; and, even if a resolution recommending an appointment were allowed to be put and carried, it would not be binding on the Council. But the most obstinate Council could not have held out long against the declared wish of a majority of the Society. There were already two signatories on the Council, and two new members were to be elected every year;* all that would have been necessary would have been to fight the elections systematically, and fill up every vacancy with a declared supporter of Russell, until the necessary majority was secured.

Oddly enough, this course was recommended to Hollond by Housman in a letter in which he refused his signature. The letter seems to me a little perverse, but it is curious and interesting enough to quote.

Dear Hollond,

I am very much obliged to you for taking the trouble to write to me about the Russell business. Russell is a great loss to the College, not merely for his eminence and celebrity, but as an agreeable and even charming person to meet; on the question of conscription I agreed with him at the time, though I now see I was wrong, and I did not feel sure that the action of the Council was wise, though his behaviour was that of a bad citizen. So far therefore I am nearly neutral: what prevents me from signing your letter is Russell's taking his name off the books of the College. After that piece of petulance he ought not even to want to come back. I cannot imagine myself doing so; and my standard of conduct is so very low that I feel I have a right to condemn those who do not come up to it.

I am writing this, not to argufy, but only in acknowledgement of your civility in writing to me. I hope I shall not be able to discover 'conscious effort' in the amiability of yourself or Hardy when I happen to sit next to you in the future. I am afraid however that if Russell did return he would meet with rudeness from some Fellows of the College, as I know he did before he left. This ought not to be, but the world is as God made it.

Your party has a clear majority, and you ought, quite

* There are five *ex officio* and eight elective members.

apart from this question, to vote yourself on to the Council as opportunities arise. There is not nearly enough young blood in it.

Yours sincerely,

A. E. HOUSMAN.

I do not understand at all what Housman means by saying that he had agreed with Russell 'on the question of conscription',* and he seems oddly concerned about minor points.

Hollond has shown me a number of other interesting letters. Langley, while supporting the memorial, thought that the appointment should be delayed 'in order to lessen the chance of an undergraduate demonstration' (presumably against Russell). The best letters are two from Whitehead. Whitehead had always been strongly on the side of fighting the war to a conclusion, and had lost a son to whom he was deeply attached; on the other hand, he had been Russell's most intimate friend. He found himself now in a terribly difficult position, and the letters in which he explains his difficulties are really moving, but too long, and perhaps too personal, to quote. It will be seen that, after much hesitation, he signed.

I conclude this section with two letters from members of the Council who had voted for Russell's dismissal and would not retract. McTaggart's is disappointing; he hints at a reasoned defence of the Council which, so far as I know, he never gave.† Parry's is at any rate straightforward.

---

* Housman's attitude to the war had been 'orthodox' throughout. He may have thought at one time that conscription was not necessary on military grounds, but that question was quite irrelevant to the controversy, and I do not know that Russell had ever expressed any opinion about it.

† Actually, McTaggart never moved an inch. He was voting against the reinstatement of conscientious objectors in their scholarships long after such an attitude had ceased to be in any sense 'popular'. There is no justification for the statement on p. 117 of Lowes Dickinson's *McTaggart*, that McTaggart 'in the difficult years after the war always played the part of a reconciler at Trinity'.

Dear Hollond, 19 Sept. 1919

After careful consideration, I do not feel myself able to sign the memorial you send me. But I should not like to say this without saying also how much I feel myself in sympathy with the general tone and spirit of the memorial. I should be very glad, when I get back, to get a chance of explaining to you my position, which is not exactly the same as that of some other Fellows who are opposed to the proposal. I do not suppose that either of us will convert the other, but discussion of such questions cannot fail to be useful in promoting the harmony of the College, which—I need not tell you—I desire as much as anyone can do. For my own part, I have no fear on this matter. I know that, whatever the decision of the College about the lectureship, I shall accept it loyally and unreservedly, and so, I am sure, will all of us.

Yours always,

J. Ellis McTaggart.

My dear Harry, 3 Oct. 1919

I did not write when I received your paper about Russell, as I wanted to think it over again, and also I was moving about a good deal. But I don't want to leave it unacknowledged till we meet again.

My first purpose in writing is to say how gratefully and heartily I appreciate the spirit in which the memorial is written. I am quite sure that if we approach this question with a real respect for each other's convictions, whatever decision we come to, we shall remain as we have so long been a house at unity with itself. Your memorial is so phrased that this spirit is thoroughly maintained; and I am most grateful for this.

I will only add that I cannot personally see my way to agreeing with the object of the memorial. The decision in which I shared was perhaps the most painful I have ever had to make: but my conviction still is that we were right: and further I cannot convince myself that reinstatement would be right. I am very sorry: but I see no escape from my conclusion. Whether you understand or not, you will in any case not misinterpret.

Ever affectionately yours,

R. St John Parry.

17. *Reinstatement and resignation*

The memorial was immediately effective, as the Council's second resolution of 12 December shows.* I do not know whether anybody voted against the resolution, but no one went so far as to record his vote. At the meeting of 16 January 1920, the Master announced that Russell had accepted the offer. He was expected to begin his lectures in October, but other factors intervened.

In July Russell applied for leave of absence for the year 1920–1921, and this was granted. He spent the year travelling and lecturing in China and Japan. On 14 January 1921 we heard that he had resigned and that his resignation had been accepted. Thus he never again occupied the post in which he had been reinstated, and few outside the College even knew of his reinstatement.

The resignation was voluntary; there had been no fresh quarrel. But Russell was approaching a crisis in his personal affairs, a divorce and a re-marriage; it would have been necessary for him to explain the whole position and to ask for leave of absence for a second year. He was afraid that such an unusual application might create a new scandal, and alienate or embarrass a good many of those who had supported him most loyally before. I had no correspondence with him myself, but I have been told what he wrote to other friends. There were two causes to which he was devoted, political and moral liberty, liberty in thought and speech and liberty in personal relations: it might be a disaster to both causes if his friends had to fight for him on both fronts at once. The lectureship, much as he would have liked to hold it, was not essential to him: it was better to put an end to controversy by resignation. Much as I regretted his decision, I thought at

* See p. 49.

57

the time, and think still, that it was probably wise. Russell showed both wisdom and consideration, and there is no point in the whole story at which I sympathize with him more whole-heartedly.

None the less it is a pity that Russell should not have returned to Trinity, if only for a year or even a term. It would have made the situation clear to the whole academic world, and prevented all the misapprehensions which have damaged the reputation of the College. As it is, the fact of reconciliation has never become at all widely known. The Council took one step in this direction in 1925, when they invited Russell to give the triennial 'Tarner Lectures' on the Philosophy of the Sciences. The invitation was accepted, and the substance of the lectures is incorporated in one of Russell's best-known books;* but few, even among philosophers, seem to have noticed the significance of the appointment. And I will end with a question. All the world of learning knows that there was a quarrel between the College and one of its most famous members: could it not be told, in language which leaves no possibility of misunderstanding, that the quarrel has since been healed?

* *The Analysis of Matter* (1927). See pp. vii–viii.

APPENDIX

List of the Fellows of Trinity on 12 *December* 1919

The names of those who supported the memorial
are printed in italics

	Age	War service
H. Jackson, Litt.D., F.B.A., O.M.	80	
H. M. Taylor, F.R.S.	77	
J. W. L. Glaisher, Sc.D., F.R.S.	71	
Very Rev. A. F. Kirkpatrick, D.D.	70	
Rev. A. H. F. Boughey	70	
W. W. R. Ball	69	
J. Ward, Sc.D., F.B.A.	*76*	
R. D. Hicks	69	
Sir R. T. Glazebrook, C.B., F.R.S.	65	
F. J. H. Jenkinson	66	
J. P. Postgate, Litt.D., F.B.A.	66	
Sir J. G. Frazer, F.B.A.	65	
Rev. R. St J. Parry, D.D.	61	
R. A. Herman	58	
J. D. Duff	59	
A. N. Whitehead, Sc.D., F.R.S.	*58*	
J. N. Langley, Sc.D., F.R.S.	*67*	
A. A. Bevan	60	
J. McT. E. McTaggart, Litt.D., F.B.A.	53	
J. W. Capstick	61	
H. McL. Innes	57	
Sir W. M. Fletcher, Sc.D., K.B.E., F.R.S.	*46*	
F. M. Cornford	*45*	*Capt., School of Musketry*
E. Harrison	*42*	*Lieut., R.N.V.R.*
G. H. Hardy, F.R.S.	*42*	
R. V. Laurence	43	
G. T. Lapsley	48	
D. A. Winstanley	*42*	
F. J. Dykes	39	

59

	Age	War service
A. S. Eddington, F.R.S.	36	
J. E. Littlewood, F.R.S.	34	Sec. Lieut., R.G.A.
H. F. Newall, F.R.S.	62	
H. A. Hollond, LL.M.	35	Major, D.A.A.G.
D. S. Robertson	34	Major, R.A.S.C.
F. G. Hopkins, F.R.S.	58	
A. E. Housman	60	
Rev. F. A. Simpson	36	C.F., R.A.C.D.
R. V. Southwell	31	Major, R.A.F.
Rev. F. R. Tennant, D.D.	53	
J. R. M. Butler	30	Major, G.S.O.(2)
E. D. Adrian, M.B., B.Ch.	30	Capt., R.A.M.C.
R. H. Fowler	30	Capt., R.M.A.
D. H. Robertson	29	Lieut., London Regt.
N. K. Adam	28	
J. Burnaby	28	Capt., London Regt.
J. Proudman	30	
P. A. Buxton	27	Capt., R.A.M.C.
O. D. Schreiner	28	Capt., S. Wales Borderers
Rev. H. F. Stewart, D.D.	56	
S. Ramanujan	31	
Sir E. Rutherford, F.R.S.	48	
G. I. Taylor, F.R.S.	33	Major, Special List
T. C. Nicholas	31	Major, R.E.
D. R. Pye	33	Capt., R.A.F.
T. H. Marshall	25	
E. A. Milne	23	Lieut., R.N.V.R.
S. Pollard	25	Sec. Lieut., R.F.A.
R. R. Sedgwick	25	

Four Fellows, K. Lucas, F.R.S., C. E. Stuart, G. B. Tatham and C. N. S. Woolf, had been killed in the war.

Postscript (5 March 1942)

In the letter from Russell (dated 20 October 1941) to which I refer in the preface, he naturally reserved the right to comment on any 'error of fact'. In a later letter (dated 20 December 1941), which I received after my manuscript was in the hands of the Press, he makes a comment, concerning the passage from *Sceptical Essays* which I quote and criticise in § 8, which falls fairly under this heading.

He tells me that the passage refers, not (as I and other Cambridge readers had supposed) to the events of 1915 described in the text, but to the original offer of a lectureship in 1910. This is indeed its obvious interpretation, the phrase 'I was invited' being much more natural in this connection; but I and other readers had been so preoccupied with the later events that the more natural interpretation had not occurred to us.

It is obvious that my mistake here destroys the force of the argument which I use in paragraph (2) at the end of § 8 (p. 30). I do not know whether there was a serious attempt to elect Russell to a Fellowship, for example under Title (ζ), in 1910, nor, if so, how it was frustrated; and it would hardly be possible now to discover the facts. But the suggestion that religious prejudice might have played an appreciable part has not the absurdity which I attributed to it, and which I think it would have had later. I still think, of course, that the passage, written as it was after Russell's reinstatement, is an unhappy one which would have been better omitted.

I have inserted this explanation here, leaving my text unaltered, in order that my statement that 'no word has been changed as the result of any suggestion from him' may remain literally true.

For EU product safety concerns, contact us at Calle de José Abascal, 56–1°,
28003 Madrid, Spain or eugpsr@cambridge.org.

www.ingramcontent.com/pod-product-compliance
Ingram Content Group UK Ltd.
Pitfield, Milton Keynes, MK11 3LW, UK
UKHW012336130625
459647UK00009B/314